中华人民共和国文化和旅游部 2020年文化和旅游发展统计公报

STATISTICAL COMMUNIQUÉ OF THE MINISTRY OF CULTURE AND TOURISM OF THE PEOPLE'S REPUBLIC OF CHINA ON CULTURAL AND TOURISM DEVELOPMENT IN 2020

中华人民共和国文化和旅游部　编

中国统计出版社
China Statistics Press

图书在版编目（CIP）数据

中华人民共和国文化和旅游部 2020 年文化和旅游发展统计公报 = Statistical Communiqu é of the Ministry of Culture and Tourism of the People' s Republic of China on Cultural and Tourism Development in 2020 : 汉英对照 / 中华人民共和国文化和旅游部编 . -- 北京 : 中国统计出版社 , 2021.9

ISBN 978-7-5037-9564-0

Ⅰ . ①中… Ⅱ . ①中… Ⅲ . ①文化发展－统计分析－公报－中国－ 2020 －汉、英②旅游业－统计分析－公报－中国－ 2020 －汉、英 Ⅳ . ① G12 ② F592

中国版本图书馆 CIP 数据核字 (2021) 第 139609 号

中华人民共和国文化和旅游部 2020 年文化和旅游发展统计公报

作　　者 / 中华人民共和国文化和旅游部
责任编辑 / 李　冲
装帧设计 / 黄　晨
出版发行 / 中国统计出版社有限公司
通信地址 / 北京市西城区月坛南街 57 号
邮政编码 / 100826
办公地址 / 北京市丰台区西三环南路甲 6 号
网　　址 / http://www.zgtjcbs.com
电　　话 /（010）63376907（发行部）
印　　刷 / 北京画中画印刷有限公司
经　　销 / 新华书店
开　　本 / 880×1230 毫米　1/16
字　　数 / 50 千字
印　　张 / 2.75
版　　别 / 2021 年 9 月第 1 版
版　　次 / 2021 年 9 月北京第 1 次印刷
定　　价 / 28.00 元

目录

CONTENTS

中华人民共和国文化和旅游部 2020 年文化和旅游发展统计公报[1]

2020 年，在党中央、国务院坚强领导下，全国文化和旅游系统坚持以习近平新时代中国特色社会主义思想为指导，全面贯彻党的十九大和十九届二中、三中、四中、五中全会精神，坚持以人民为中心的工作导向，坚持稳中求进工作总基调，坚持新发展理念，努力克服新冠肺炎疫情严重影响，强化政策应对力度，扎实做好“六稳”工作、全面落实“六保”任务，我国文化建设和旅游发展取得积极进展。

一、机构和人员

2020 年末，纳入统计范围的全国各类文化和旅游单位[2]34.16 万个，比上年末减少 0.63 万个。其中，各级文化和旅游部门所属单位 66555 个，减少 221 个；从业人员 69.98 万人，增加 0.46 万人。

二、艺术创作演出

2020 年，文化和旅游系统紧紧围绕举旗帜、聚民心、育新人、兴文化、展形象的使命任务，坚持以人民为中心的创作导向，推动舞台艺术和美术繁荣发展。紧扣全面建成小康社会、纪念中国人民志愿军抗美援朝出国作战 70 周年和纪念中国人民抗日战争暨世界反法西斯战争胜利 75 周年等关键时间节点，组织引导创作复排文艺精品力作，涌现歌剧《红船》《同心结》、舞剧《英雄儿女》《骑兵》、京剧《奇袭白虎团》、彩调剧《新刘三姐》、话剧《三湾，那一夜》等一批优秀作品。

新冠肺炎疫情爆发后，文化和旅游部第一时间在“中国艺术头条”微信公众号推出“艺术战‘疫’”专栏，共发布 30 期 291 件艺术作品，阅读量近两亿人次，带动了全国文艺界以“艺”战“疫”的热潮。推出“文艺中国”快手号，累计点击量 2.1 亿。举办全国舞台艺术优秀剧目网络展演，观看互动人次超 11.7 亿；全国基层戏曲院团网络会演观看人次超 8500 万。组织国家京剧院及全国 18 家优秀京剧院团开展“京剧的夏天”线上公益展演，收看人数达 7800 万余人次。举办 2020 年戏曲百戏（昆山）

盛典，展演 116 个剧种，演出大戏 22 台、折子戏组台 20 场，戏曲晚会 1 场，3 年实现了 348 个戏曲剧种的“大团圆”。

2020 年末，全国共有艺术表演团体[3]17581 个，比上年末减少 214 个；从业人员 43.69 万人，增加 2.44 万人。其中各级文化和旅游部门所属艺术表演团体 1973 个，占 11.2%，从业人员 10.75 万人，占 24.6%。

全年全国艺术表演团体共演出 223.20 万场，比上年下降 24.8%；国内观众 8.90 亿人次，下降 27.6%；演出收入 86.63 亿元，下降 31.7%。

全年全国文化和旅游部门所属艺术表演团体共组织政府采购公益演出 13.38 万场，比上年下降 14.9%；观众 0.86 亿人次，下降 27.9%。

表 1 2011-2020 年全国艺术表演团体基本情况

年　份	机构数（个）	从业人员（万人）	演出场次（万场）	国内演出观众人次（亿人次）	演出收入（亿元）
2011	7055	22.66	154.72	7.46	52.67
2012	7321	24.20	135.02	8.28	64.15
2013	8180	26.09	165.11	9.01	82.07
2014	8769	26.29	173.91	9.10	75.70
2015	10787	30.18	210.78	9.58	93.93
2016	12301	33.29	230.60	11.81	120.86
2017	15742	40.30	293.57	12.47	147.68
2018	17123	41.64	312.46	11.76	152.27
2019	17795	41.25	296.80	12.30	126.78
2020	17581	43.69	223.20	8.90	86.63

2020 年末，全国共有艺术表演场馆 2770 个，比上年末增加 54 个；观众坐席数 187.89 万个，增长 3.3%；全年共演映 58.80 万场，比上年下降 54.2%；观众 6064.67 万人次，下降 51.7%。公有制艺术表演场馆 1208 个，比上年末减少 75 个；全年共演映 24.39 万场，比上年下降 64.26%；观众人次 2187.92 万人次，下降 61.47%。文化和旅游部门所属艺术表演场馆 1111 个，比上年末减少 91 个，全年艺术演出 3.38 万场次，比上年下降 45.4%；观众人次 1072.13 万人次，下降 58.7%。

2020 年末，全国共有美术馆 618 个，比上年末增加 59 个；从业人员 5467 人，增加 451 人。全年共举办展览5988次，比上年下降17.6%；参观人次2186.76万人次，下降47.1%。

三、公共服务

2020年，文化和旅游系统进一步贯彻落实《中华人民共和国公共文化服务保障法》《中华人民共和国公共图书馆法》，配合全国人大开展公共文化服务保障法执法检查。开展全国“乡村春晚”集中展演暨网络联动活动，全国24个省（区、市）88场“乡村春晚”参加活动，线上参与人次达1320.5万。启动小康生活主题美术创作征集展示活动，实施“乡村网红”培育计划，引领乡风文明建设。持续实施“春雨工程”“阳光工程”等重大文化和旅游志愿服务项目，组织开展“央视频·文化志愿者专列”贫困地区文化和旅游资源推介等活动。推进《旅游厕所质量等级的划分与评定》等国家标准制修订工作，全年新建、改扩建旅游厕所2.03万座，超额完成新三年行动计划目标任务，加快推进旅游厕所电子地图上线，14.5万座厕所已在手机APP进行标注。

（一）公共图书馆[4]

2020年末，全国共有公共图书馆3212个，比上年末增加16个；从业人员57980人，增加184人。其中具有高级职称人员7053人，占12.2%；具有中级职称人员18868人，占32.5%。

2020年末，全国公共图书馆实际使用房屋建筑面积1785.77万平方米，比上年末增长12.2%；全国图书总藏量[5]117929.99万册，增长6.1%；阅览室坐席数126.47万个，增长6.2%；计算机226234台，增加419台；其中供读者使用的电子阅览终端143714万台，减少2022台。

2020年末，全国平均每万人公共图书馆建筑面积126.49平方米，比上年末增加5.09平方米，全国人均图书藏量0.84册，增加0.05册；全年全国人均购书费1.60元，减少0.08元。

图1 2011-2020年全国公共图书馆人均资源情况

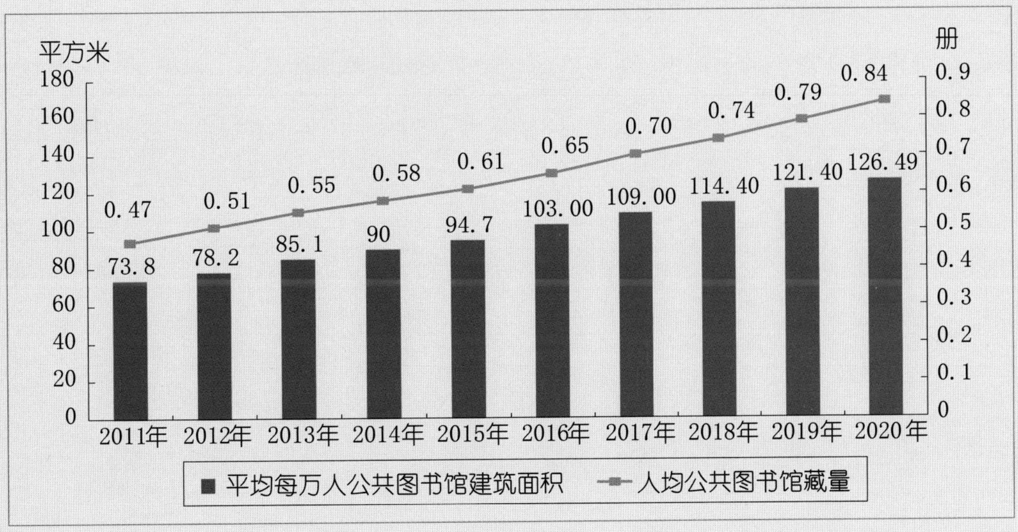

全年公共图书馆发放借书证[6]10251.31 万个，比上年增长 18.8%；总流通人次[7]54145.81 万，比上年下降 39.9%；书刊文献外借 42087.15 万册次，下降 31.4%；外借人次 17466.62 万，下降 34.4%。全年共为读者举办各种活动 150713 次，比上年下降 23.0%；参加人次 9279.33 万，下降 21.3%。

图 2 2011–2020 年全国公共图书馆总流通人次及书刊外借册次

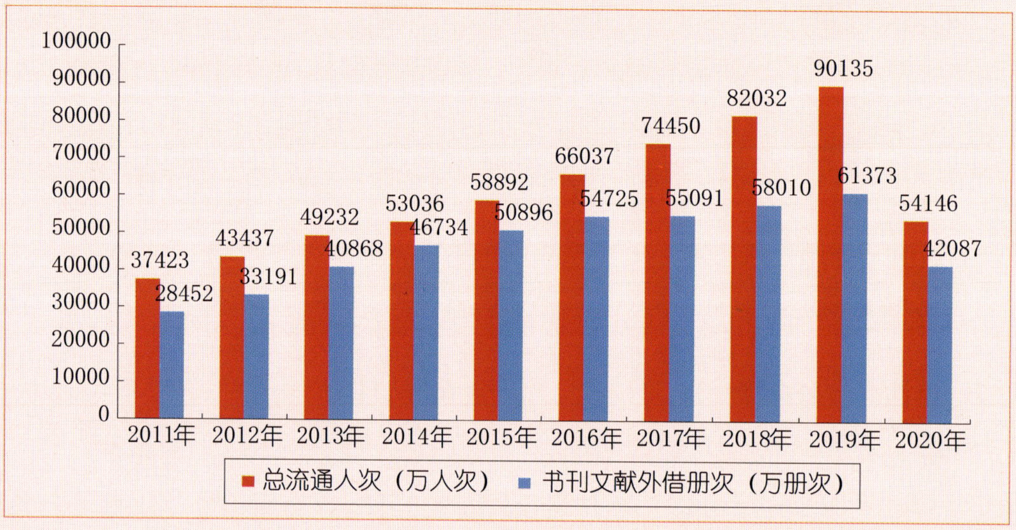

2020 年末，全国共 2397 个县（市、区）建成图书馆总分馆制，406 个公共图书馆组建理事会。

（二）群众文化机构[8]

2020 年末，全国共有群众文化机构 43687 个，比上年末减少 386 个。其中乡镇综合文化站 32825 个，减少 705 个。年末全国群众文化机构从业人员 185076 人，比上年末减少 4992 人。其中具有高级职称的人员 7075 人，占 3.8%；具有中级职称人员 17969 人，占 9.7%。

2020 年末，全国群众文化机构实际使用房屋建筑面积 4677.88 万平方米，比上年末增长 3.5%；业务用房面积 3387.86 万平方米，增长 2.8%。年末全国平均每万人群众文化设施建筑面积 331.32 平方米，增长 2.7%。

图 3 2011-2020 年全国平均每万人群众文化设施建筑面积

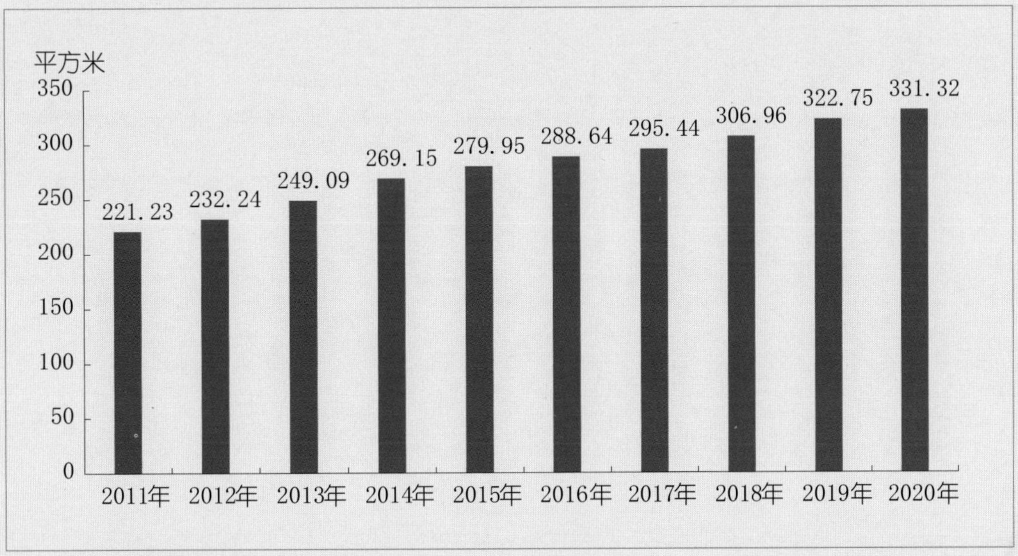

全年全国群众文化机构共组织开展各类文化活动[9]192.65 万场次，比上年下降 21.4%；服务人次 56327.04 万人次，下降 28.4%。

2020 年末，全国群众文化机构共有馆办文艺团体[10]9489 个，演出 12.08 万场，观众 6675.84 万人次。由文化馆（站）指导的群众业余文艺团体 45.46 万个，馆办老年大学 698 个。

表 2 2020 年全国群众文化机构活动开展情况

项 目	总量		比上年增长（%）	
	活动次数（万次）	服务人次（万人次）	活动次数	服务人次
各项活动总计	**192.65**	**56327.04**	**-21.4**	**-28.4**
其中：文艺活动	108.89	43134.40	-19.9	-28.3
训练班	66.89	3931.26	-24.8	-27.3
展览	13.79	8692.36	-15.9	-30.3
公益性讲座	3.06	565.74	-20.2	-20.4

2020 年末，全国共建成村级综合性文化服务中心 575384 个，2578 个县（市、区）建成文化馆总分馆制，394 个文化馆组建理事会。

四、市场管理和发展

2020 年，文化和旅游部进一步支持引导文化市场经营单位改进服务、转变形象，不断提升市场监管水平。起草制定《在线旅游经营服务管理暂行规定》《文化和旅游部关于深化“放管服”改革促进演出市场繁荣发展的通知》等制度规范性文件，为市场监管提供政策保障。修订印发演出管理有关工作指引，建立完善卡拉 OK 歌曲内容自审机制，实现游戏游艺设备内容审核“一网通办”和设备全流程电子标识管理。健全旅游安全管理体制机制，组织开展 2020 年旅游安全云课堂培训，指导地方文化和旅游部门和企业开展应急培训和演练 40 余次，培训人员近 3 万人次。进一步完善文化和旅游市场新型监管机制，加快建立以信用为基础的新型监管机制，深入开展信用评价规范研究，推进文化和旅游市场“失信名单”管理常态化，研究推进文化市场服务质量提升工作，落实旅游服务质量提升计划，开展第三方评估，进一步提升政策效能。完善星评制度，推进旅游住宿业标准化工作。组织开展全国导游资格考试和中高级导游等级考试，实施导游专业素养研培计划。

2020 年末，全国共有文化市场经营单位[11]20.89 万家，从业人员 160.91 万人，营业收入 9967.49 亿元，营业利润 1699.70 亿元。其中，娱乐场所 6.54 万个，从业人员 53.23 万人，营业收入 419.25 亿元，营业利润 5.33 亿元。互联网上网服务营业场所 10.62 万个，从业人员 24.71 万人，营业收入 181.53 亿元。演出市场单位 2.23 万个，从业人员 49.52 万人，营业收入 2157.50 亿元，营业利润 351.15 亿元。艺术品经营机构 0.53 万个，从业人员 1.94 万人，营业收入 71.99 亿元，营业利润 9.29 亿元。经营性互联网文化单位 0.97 万家，从业人员 31.49 万人，营业收入 7137.22 亿元，营业利润 1331.13 亿元。

根据 31074 家旅行社统计数据显示，全年旅行社营业收入 2389.69 亿元，营业利润 −69.15 亿元，直接从业人员 32.25 万人。

根据 8423 家星级饭店统计数据显示，全年星级饭店营业收入 1221.53 亿元，平均房价 313.91 元／间夜，平均出租率 39.0%。

2020 年，文化和旅游部深入推进文化市场综合执法改革，持续加强文化、文物、出版、广播电视、电影、旅游等各类市场综合执法，以整合组建文化市场综合执法队伍为重点，积极推进各项改革任务落实。省级层面，所有省（区、市）印发改革实施意见，所有省（区）文化和旅游行政部门成立文化市场综合执法监督局（处）市级层面，99.8% 的市（州、盟）完成文化市场综合执法队伍与旅游市场执法队伍整合，85.5% 的设区市整合区级执法队伍组建市级执法队伍，4.1% 的设区市撤销市级执法队伍保留区级执法队伍。县级层面，95.9% 的县（市、区）完成文化市场综合执法队伍与旅游市场执法队伍的整合，深入落实“局队合一”管理体制。全年开展各类线上线下培训 25 期，累计培训 3 万余人次。指导监督各地开展执法资格专业考试 9 场次，完成 4239 人执法资格和证件信息采集汇总。

2020 年，文化和旅游部全面加强文化和旅游市场执法，线下开展四轮文化和旅游市场“体检式”暗访评估，范围基本覆盖全国各省。配合网信办等部门开展网络直播行业专项整治行动，排查具有网络表演业务的手机直播应用软件。查处违法违规互联网文化活动，检查各类互联网文化经营单位，清理下线各类含有违规内容的网络文化产品。加强假日旅游市场执法，部署执法队伍巡查景区等 47 万余次，及时处置问题 1100 余个。严查“直播带货”旅游产品，查处违规旅行社和网店 30 余家。开展第一批旅游市场集中办案，集中查处一批旅游市场典型案件。开展重大案件评选，评选 87 件 2019−2020 年度文化市场综合执法重大案件。联合中央宣传部、公安部、最高检等部门督办 42 起社会影响恶劣的重大案件。推进全国文化市场技术监管与服务平台建设应用，全年通过该平台进行举报登记 8827 件、办结 6725 件；累计发起日常检查 316.41 万件，出动检查 1088.94 万人次；建议立案 2.09 万件，累计办结案件 2.84 万件。

五、资源开发和利用

2020 年，文化和旅游部成立中华文化资源普查工作领导小组，制定中华文化资源公共数据库建设方案、数据规范和旅游资源普查工作技术规程，开展文化和旅游资源普查示范项目，推出 22 家国家 5A 级旅游景区和 15 家国家级旅游度假区，公布第二批 97 家国家全域旅游示范区和 680 个全国乡村旅游重点村名单。开展“心灵四季 · 美丽中国”“感受美丽家乡、发现户外精彩”系列宣传推广活动、全国冰雪旅游宣传推广活动和“最美风景在路上”自驾游系列推广活动，支持黄河、长城、长江等旅游推广联盟开展跨区域主题推广。应对疫情影响及时开设“乡村旅游面对面直播课堂”，完成 49 期课堂，累计学习超过 70 万人次。组织编印《“三区三州”旅游大环线自驾路书》，推动开设“三区三州 · 旅游大环线客源援藏专列”，积极发挥旅游助力脱贫攻坚积极作用，2.26 万个旅游扶贫重点村全部脱贫。深入实施全国红色旅游五好讲解员培养项目，举办红色旅游发展典型案例征集展示活动、第十届全国大学生红色旅游创意策划大赛、2020 中国红色旅游博览会、红色旅游云课堂、“红色之旅 壮美兵团”等活动，红色旅游发展持续向好。

图 4 2011−2020 年国内旅游发展情况

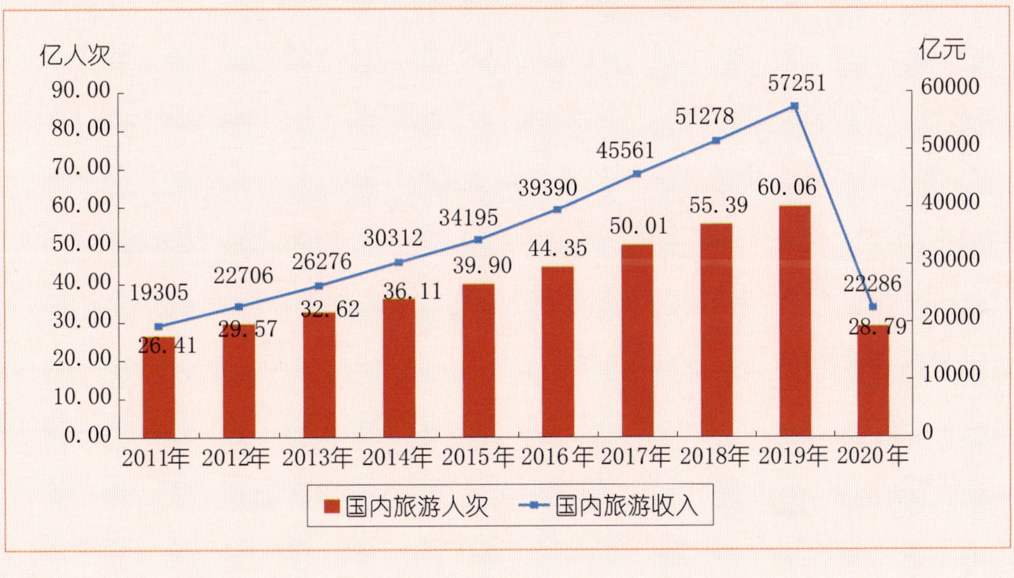

2020年末，全国共有A级旅游景区13332个，比上年末增加930个。其中，5A级旅游景区302个，增加22个；4A级旅游景区4030个，增加310个；3A级旅游景区6931个，增加733个。

2020年，全年国内旅游人数28.79亿人次，比上年同期下降52.1%。国内旅游收入2.23万亿元，同比下降61.1%。

六、产业与科技

2020年，文化和旅游部制定出台《文化和旅游部关于推动数字文化产业高质量发展的意见》，联合发展改革委等部门印发《关于促进消费扩容提质加快形成强大国内市场的实施意见》《关于支持新业态新模式健康发展激活消费市场带动扩大就业的意见》，积极培育新业态新消费新模式。联合发展改革委、财政部公布第一批15个国家文化和旅游消费示范城市、60个国家文化和旅游消费试点城市名单。

2020年，文化和旅游部新命名9家国家级文化产业示范园区，授予18家园区创建资格，年末全国共有国家级文化产业示范园区19家。联合工业和信息化部等部门制定印发《关于健全支持中小企业发展制度的若干意见》。联合国家开发银行等6家金融机构遴选320个全国文化和旅游投融资项目，项目总投资额6194.1亿元。举办包括7期精品项目交流对接会、大运河重点项目投融资对接会在内的各类投融资对接活动，共推介项目452个，总投资额3405.9亿元。与中国工商银行签署协议，新增1000亿元纾困复产贷款授信额度。依托中国银联对2.4万家文化和旅游消费场所进行移动支付能力提升。举办“一带一路”文化产业和旅游产业国际合作论坛，与日本、韩国联合主办第13届中日韩文化产业论坛，征集遴选2020年“一带一路”文化产业和旅游产业国际合作项目45个。

根据国家统计局统计，2020年全国规模以上文化及相关产业企业实现营业收入98514亿元，按可比口径比上年增长2.2%。

2020年，文化和旅游部完成“科技助力经济2020”国家重点专项、国家文化和旅游科技创新工程项目、文化和旅游部重点实验室资助项目遴选工作。故宫博物院获批科技部第二批“一带一路”联合实验室。发布文化和旅游国家标准、行业标准13项。公布第四批全国旅游标准化示范单位28个，年末全国旅游标准化示范单位共有198家。加快推进一体化在线政务服务平台部省试点对接。立项国家社科基金艺术学项目242项，加强对黄河文化、长江文化等选题研究。开展全国艺术职业院校“立德树人”校园艺术作品展等活动。

七、文化遗产保护利用

2020年，文化和旅游系统、文物系统进一步贯彻落实《关于加强文物保护利用改革的若干意见》《关于实施革命文物保护利用工程（2018—2022）的意见）》《关于加强石窟寺保护利用工作的指导意见》，健全不可移动文物保护机制、文物保护工程管理制度体系，推进中华文明探源工程、“考古中国”重大项目和中国文化基因研究相关工作，启动南水北调东线二期考古和文物保护工程。国家文物局深入实施革命文物保护利用工程，公布第二批革命文物保护利用片区分县名单，共 22 个片区，涉及 31 个省 228 个市 988 个县。推动各地制定革命文物保护利用专项规划、公布革命文物名录等，加强革命文物保护项目的组织实施，共批复国保、馆藏一级革命文物保护项目 246 个，推出“武汉革命文物线上展示月”“遵循先烈足迹”等主题活动。全国古籍普查完成汉文古籍 270 万余部。

2020 年末，全国共有各类文物机构 11314 个，比上年末增加 752 个，其中，文物保护管理机构 3373 个，占 29.8%；博物馆[12]5452 个，占 48.2%。年末全国文物机构从业人员 17.57 万人，比上年末增加 1.34 万人。其中高级职称 11072 人，占 6.3%；中级职称 22165 人，占 12.6%。

图 5 2011-2020 年全国文物机构及从业人员情况

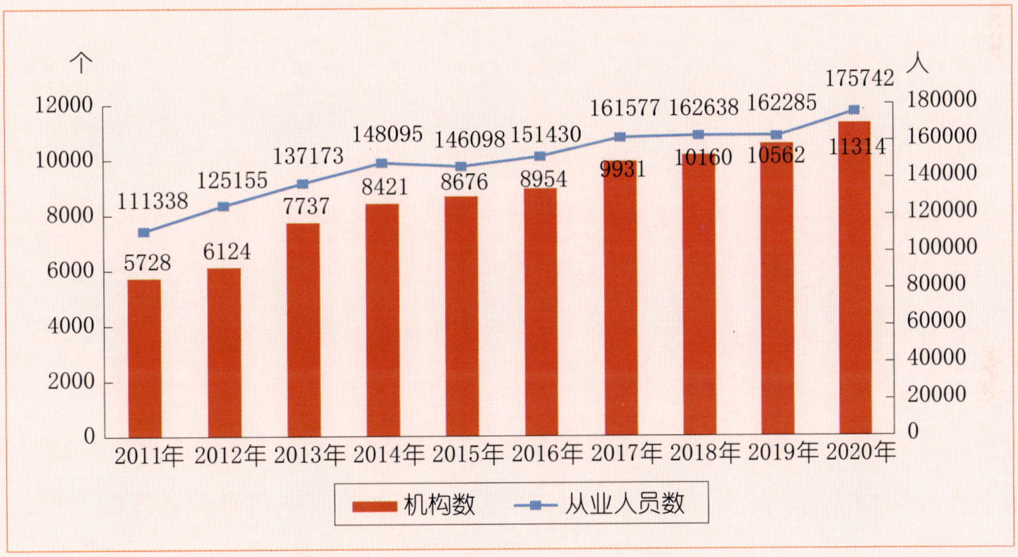

2020 年末，全国文物机构藏品 5089.10 万件 / 套，其中，博物馆文物藏品 4319.09 万件 / 套，占文物藏品总量的 84.9%。

全年全国各类文物机构共举办陈列展览 28924 个，比上年减少 1778 个。其中，基本陈列[13]16259 个，增加 1235 个；临时展览[14]12665 个，减少 3013 个。接待观众 61631.70 万人次，比上年下降 53.2%，其中未成年人 13564.08 万人次，下降 57.1%，占参观总人数的 22.0%。博物馆接待观众 52652.35 万人次，比上年减少 53.1%，占文物机构接待观众总数的 85.4%。

2020 年，“太极拳”“送王船”项目成功列入联合国教科文组织人类非物质文化遗产代表作名录。普洱景迈山古茶林文化景观、海上丝绸之路、丝绸之路南亚廊道、中蒙俄万里茶道申遗工作有序推进。文化和旅游部完成第五批国家级非遗代表性项目初评工作，列入联合国教科文组织非遗名录

图 6 2011-2020 年全国文物机构接待观众人次及未成年人观众人次

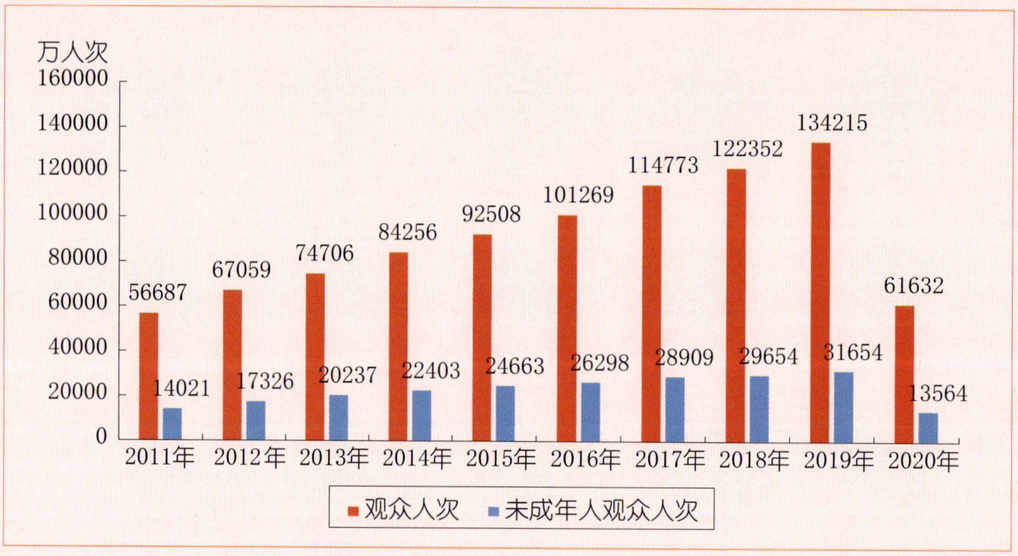

（册）项目保护工作实现规范化管理。深入实施中国传统工艺振兴计划、中国非遗传承人群研培计划和国家级非遗代表性传承人认定与管理办法，对 249 名国家级非遗代表性传承人进行记录。建立黄河流域、大运河沿线非遗保护协同机制，组织实施黄河流域非遗调查，试点设立近 40 家非遗曲艺书场，设立河洛文化、景德镇陶瓷文化生态保护实验区。举办第六届中国非遗博览会、2020 年“文化和自然遗产日”非遗宣传展示活动、“全国非遗曲艺周”“非遗过大年 文化进万家”活动，支持各地举办“非遗购物节”、杭州工艺周、中国纺织非遗大会等品牌活动，推进“非遗进校园、进社区、进景区”，发布 12 条全国非遗主题旅游线路。

2020 年末，全国共有国务院公布国家级非遗代表性项目 1372 项，共有文化和旅游部认定国家级非遗代表性传承人 3068 名。全国列入联合国教科文组织人类非物质文化遗产代表作名录（名册）42 项，位居世界第一。

年末全国共有非物质文化遗产保护机构 2455 个，从业人员 16444 人。全年全国各类非物质文化遗产保护机构举办演出 56117 场，比上年下降 22.0%；举办民俗活动 12227 次，下降 28.0%；举办展览 16174 场，下降 17.4%。

八、对外及对港澳台交流

2020 年，文化和旅游部持续推进“一带一路”建设，举办“云聚荟”直播盛典、全球博物馆珍藏展示在线接力、丝绸之路文献展览等活动，全面深化双边合作机制，开展部级双边访问、召开高级别会议 16 次，推动与匈牙利、希腊等 7 国签署合作执行计划或谅解备忘录，举办与意大利、沙特等 6 国建交周年庆祝活动，开展对尼日利亚等非洲 8 国人力资源培训班等项目。参与金砖国家、二十国集团以及联合国教科文组织文化部长网络会议等重要会议活动 32 次，稳步推进世界旅游联盟总部建设。

文化和旅游部持续提升“美丽中国”整体形象，举办“欢乐春节”活动近200场，组织参加线上日本旅游博览会、英国伦敦国际旅游交易会等国际展会，举办“丝路交响”云端音乐会、“意会中国”亚非当代音乐论坛等线上交流活动，统筹指导海外中国文化中心和驻外旅游办事处开展全球联动的“云·游中国”系列线上活动和“天涯共此时——中秋节”线上文化周，举办各类活动2200余项。

文化和旅游部持续深化对港澳台文化和旅游工作，印发粤港澳大湾区文化和旅游发展规划，召开“两岸旅游交流线上座谈会”“两岸文化交流线上座谈会”。举办“国家艺术院团（澳门）演出季”“金瓯无缺——纪念台湾光复75周年文献展”“艺海流金·美好安徽”“情系三江源·大美青海情”等活动。实施“港澳青少年知行计划”“台湾青少年春节习俗研习营”等青少年交流项目，举办港澳青少年游学推广活动暨内地游学联盟大会，不断做深做实对港澳台文化品牌。

2020年，在匈牙利、约旦、科威特新设3个海外中国文化中心。截至2020年末，在全球设有45家海外中国文化中心，20家驻外旅游办事处。此外，在香港设有亚洲旅游交流中心，在台湾设有海峡两岸旅游交流协会台北办事处、高雄办事分处。全年对外、对港澳台演出团体达947个团次，参与交流人员12552人次。

九、资金投入

2020年，文化和旅游部全年落实文化和旅游部部门预算59.51亿元，落实中央补助地方转移支付资金54.92亿元。运用全覆盖审计、绩效管理等手段，提高资金资产使用管理效能。国家美术馆工程、中国工艺美术馆工程（暂定名）、“平安故宫”工程等重大文化设施建设项目取得积极进展。

图7 2011-2020年全国人均文化和旅游事业费及增速情况

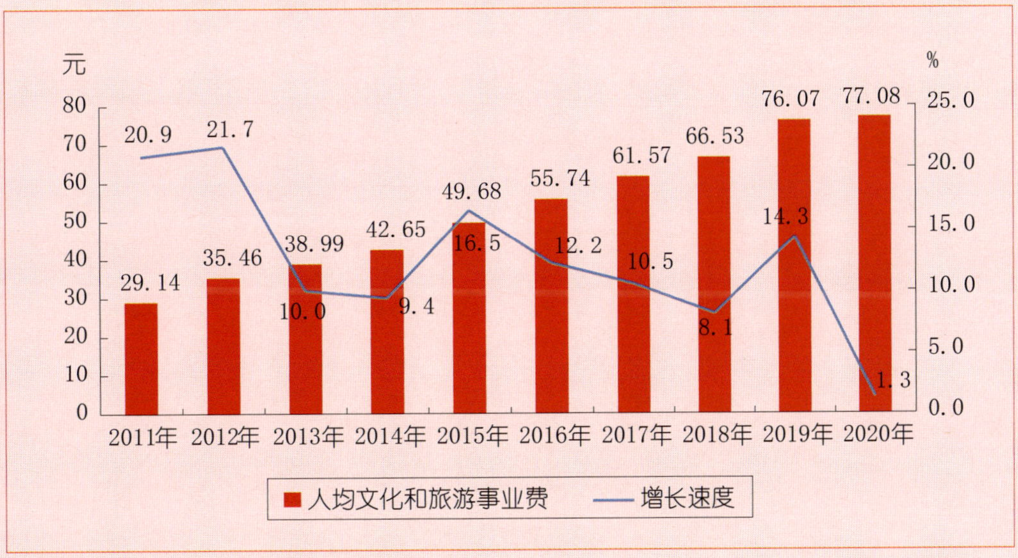

2020年，全国文化和旅游事业费[15]1088.26亿元，比上年增加22.5亿元，增长2.1%；全国人均文化和旅游事业费77.08元，比上年增加1.01元，增长1.3%。

全国文化和旅游事业费中，县以上文化和旅游事业费500.98亿元，占46.0%，比重比上年下降2.5个百分点；县及县以下文化和旅游事业费587.28亿元，占54.0%，比重提高了2.5个百分点。东部地区[16]文化和旅游事业费491.62亿元，占45.1%，比重提高了0.2个百分点。中部地区文化和旅游事业费269.78亿元，占24.8%，比重降低了0.1个百分点。西部地区文化和旅游事业费301.64亿元，占27.7%，比重提高了1.6个百分点。

全年全国文物事业费[17]400.20亿元，比上年减少15.21亿元，下降3.7%。

表3 全国文化和旅游事业费按城乡和区域分布情况

项目		1995	2000	2005	2010	2015	2018	2019	2020
总量(亿元)	全国	33.4	63.2	133.8	323.1	686.0	928.3	1065.8	1088.3
	#县以上	24.4	46.3	98.1	206.7	352.8	425.0	517.7	501.0
	县及县以下	9.0	16.9	35.7	116.4	330.1	503.4	548.1	587.3
	#东部地区	13.4	28.9	64.4	143.4	287.9	416.2	478.2	491.6
	中部地区	9.5	15.1	30.6	78.7	164.3	232.7	265.3	269.8
	西部地区	8.3	13.7	27.6	85.8	193.9	242.9	278.0	301.6
所占比重(%)	全国	100.0	100.0	100.0	100.0	100.0	100.0	100.0	100.0
	#县以上	73.2	73.4	73.3	64.0	51.7	45.8	48.5	46.0
	县及县以下	26.8	26.7	26.7	36.0	48.3	54.2	51.5	54.0
	#东部地区	40.2	45.7	48.1	44.4	42.1	44.8	44.9	45.1
	中部地区	28.6	23.8	22.9	24.3	24.1	25.1	24.9	24.8
	西部地区	24.9	21.7	20.6	26.6	28.4	26.2	26.1	27.7

注释：

[1] 本公报中各项数据为初步统计数据。各项统计数据均未包括香港特别行政区、澳门特别行政区和台湾省。部分数据因四舍五入的原因，存在着与分项合计不等的情况。

[2] 文化和旅游单位是指全国各级文化和旅游部门主办的或实行行业管理的文化机构，不含各级新闻出版、广播影视等部门门主办或管理的机构。根据现行的统计制度，各级文化和旅游部门主办单位（如公共图书馆、文化馆、文化站、博物馆、公有制艺术表演团体、公有制艺术表演场馆等）全部纳入统计范围，实行行业管理的文化和旅游单位中，包括娱乐场所和互联网上网服务营业场所、非公有制艺术表演团体、非公有制艺术表演场馆、经营性互联网文化单位、艺术品经营机构和演出经纪机构和 A 级景区、星级饭店和旅行社数据。

[3] 艺术表演团体指由文化和旅游部主办或实行行业管理（经文化行政部审批并领取营业性演出许可证），专门从事表演艺术等活动的各类专业艺术表演团体。

[4] 公共图书馆是指由各级文化和旅游部主办的、面向社会公众开放并提供科学、文化等各种知识普及教育的机构。

[5] 公共图书馆总藏量指已编目的古籍、图书、期刊和报纸的合订本、手册、手稿，以及缩微制品、录像带、录音带、光盘等视听文献资料数量之和，不包括电子图书。

[6] 公共图书馆发放的借书证数是指由公共图书馆发放，并在当年内使用过至少一次的借书证数。

[7] 公共图书馆总流通人次是指本年度内到图书馆场馆接受图书馆服务的总人次，包括借阅书刊、咨询问题，以及参加各类读者活动等。

[8] 群众文化机构是指各级文化和旅游部主办的开展群众文化活动的场所，主要包括文化馆（含综合性文化中心、群众艺术馆）、文化站。

[9] 群众文化机构组织开展活动是指组织文艺活动、举办训练班、举办展览和组织公益性讲座总和。

[10] 群众文化机构馆办文艺团体指由本馆人员组成的为群众提供文艺演出的演出团队。

[11] 文化市场经营单位指经审批或备案并领取相关许可或备案文件的、从事文化经营和文化服务活动的机构。按照现行统计制度，文化市场经营单位统计范围包括娱乐场所和互联网上网服务营业场所、非公有制艺术表演团体、非公有制艺术表演场馆、经营性互联网文化单位、艺术品经营机构和演出经纪机构。

[12] 博物馆指为了研究、教育、欣赏的目的，收藏、保护、展示人类活动和自然环境的见证物，向公众开放，非营利性、永久性社会服务机构，包括以博物馆（院）、纪念馆（舍）、科技馆、陈列馆等专有名称开展活动的单位。

[13] 基本陈列指在本馆布置陈列、地点固定、时间较长的展出。

[14] 临时展览指在本机构内设置，由本馆设计布陈，形式比较多样的展出。

[15] 文化和旅游事业费是指区域内各级财政对文化和旅游系统主办单位的经费投入总和。根据现行统计口径，文化和旅游事业费不包括各级文化和旅游行政部门的行政运行经费。

[16] 东部地区包括北京、天津、辽宁、上海、江苏、浙江、福建、山东、广东；中部地区包括河北、山西、吉林、黑龙江、安徽、江西、河南、湖北、湖南、海南；西部地区包括内蒙古、广西、重庆、四川、贵州、云南、西藏、陕西、甘肃、青海、宁夏、新疆。

[17] 文物事业费是指区域内各级财政对文物事业的经费投入总和。一般包括博物馆、文物保护管理机构等文物事业单位的财政拨款（不含基建拨款）及文物部门所属企业的财政补贴。

Statistical Communiqué of the Ministry of Culture and Tourism of the People's Republic of China on Cultural and Tourism Development in 2020[1]

In 2020, under the firm leadership of CPC Central Committee and the State Council of China, and with the guidance of Xi Jinping Thought on Socialism with Chinese Characteristics for A New Era, all governmental cultural and tourism departments in China have implemented and put into practice the the guiding principles from the 19th CPC National Congress, the 2nd, 3rd, 4th and 5th Plenary Sessions of the 19th CPC Central Committee, and worked in a steady and progressive way with China's new development philosophy as the guidance and people at the center of their work. As they overcome the impact of the COVID-19, developed more adaptable policies, and strived to ensure stability on the six fronts and security in the six areas, China's culture and tourism sectors embraced new progresses.

I. Institution and Employment

341,600 national cultural and tourism units[2] were brought into the statistical range by the end of 2020, 6,300 less than the number of the previous year. Among them, 66,555 units were affiliated to government cultural and tourism departments, 221 less than those of the past year, with 699,800 employees, 4,600 persons more than those of the previous year.

II. Performing Arts

In 2020, China's cultural and tourism administrations upheld the mission to hold high the banners of Marxism and socialism with Chinese characteristics, unite the people, foster a new generation capable of shouldering the mission of national rejuvenation, celebrate the best of Chinese culture and resent a true, multidimensional, and panoramic view of China to the world. They put people at the center as they worked to boost performing arts an fine arts. Productions of excellence were created or recreated under the guidance of the Ministry to commemorate important occasions such as completing the task of building a moderately prosperous society in all respects, the 70th anniversary of the Chinese People's Volunteers army entering the Democratic People's Republic of Korea to help in the war to resist US aggression and the 75th anniversary of the victory of the Chinese People's War of Resistance Against Japanese Aggression and the World Anti-Fascist War, and the repertoire included operas *The Red Boat* and *True Love Knot*, dance drama *Heroes and Heroines* and *The Rider*, Peking opera *Raid on the White Tiger Regiment,* caidiao opera *Liu Sanjie,* and play *The Whole Night's Meeting in Sanwan.*

After the outbreak of the Covid-19 pandemic, the Ministry timely launched a special "arts against virus" topic on the China Arts Headline official Wechat account to inspire artists and writers in China to fight the pandemic with art and culture. 30 issues of this topic were published to present 291 art works, with the total clicks reaching 200 million. The Ministry also created "Chinese Culture and Arts" Kuaishou account, which attracted over 210 million clicks. With the Ministry as the organizer, the Online Showcases of Excellent Performing Arts Productions of China, Online Shows of Works Presented by Local Opera Troupes, and "Summer of Peking Opera" online shows presented by China National Peking Opera Company and other 18 outstanding Peking opera companies in China were held, attracting interactive audiences of over 1.17 billion, over 85 million and over 78 million respectively. The Ministry also organized the 2020 Chinese Opera Gala (Kunshan) to celebrate 116 local operas through 22 complete productions, 20 shows of various opera highlights, and 1 evening gala. This event, which has been held for three annual sessions, brought together and put on stage all 348 local operas of China.

By the end of the year, the number of art performance troupes[3] reached 17,581, a decrease of 214 over the end of the previous year; that of the professionals reached 436,900 with an increase of 24,400. Of them, the number of art performance troupes managed by cultural and tourism departments at all levels reached 1,973, accounting for 11.2% of the total with 107,500 professionals, which is 24.6% of the total.

In 2020, all arts troupes in China presented 2.2320 million performances, a decrease of 24.8% over the previous year; the domestic audiences reached 890 million, down by 27.6%. The total performing arts box office was 8.663 billion yuan, down by 31.7%.

The amount of government-purchased non-profit performances presented by art performance troupes affiliated to official cultural and tourism departments throughout the year was 133,800, with audience attendance of 86 million, down by 14.9% and 27.9% respectively.

Table 1: General information of art troupes nationwide in 2011-2020

Year	Number of institutions (unit)	Number of employees (ten thousand)	Number of shows (ten thousand)	Number of domestic audience attendances (one hundred million person-time)	Shows' box office (one hundred million yuan)
2011	7055	22.66	154.72	7.46	52.67
2012	7321	24.20	135.02	8.28	64.15
2013	8180	26.09	165.11	9.01	82.07
2014	8769	26.29	173.91	9.10	75.70
2015	10787	30.18	210.78	9.58	93.93
2016	12301	33.29	230.60	11.81	120.86
2017	15742	40.30	293.57	12.47	147.68
2018	17123	41.64	312.46	11.76	152.27
2019	17795	41.25	296.80	12.30	126.78
2020	17581	43.69	223.20	8.90	86.63

By the end of the year, the number of venues of the performing arts amounted to 2,770, 54 more than those of the previous year, with 1,878,900 seats, up by 3.3%. 588,000 art performances were held throughout the year, down by 54.2% over the previous year; the audience reached 60.6467 million, a decrease of 51.7%. Among the venues, 1,208 are state-owned, down by 75 compared to that of previous year. 243,900 performances were held at these venues, down by 64.3%, with the size of audience of 21,879 million, a decrease of 61.47%. 33,800 performances were held in state-owned venues affiliated to the cultural and tourism departments throughout the year, down by 45.4%; the number of such venues is 1,111, a decrease of 91 compared with that of the previous year; the size of audience reached 10.7213 million, a decrease of 58.7%.

By the end of 2020, there were 618 art museums in China, 59 more than those of the previous year, with 5,467 employees, 451 more than the previous year. 5,988 exhibitions were presented by these museums year-round, down by 17.6%, attracting 21.8676 million visitor attendances, down by 47.1% over the number of the previous year.

III. Public Cultural Service

In 2020, China's cultural and tourism administrations have taken further steps to implement the laws on the public cultural service guarantee and on public libraries of the People' s Republic of China, and cooperated with National People's Congress in its inspection campaign of the implementation of the Public Cultural Service Guarantee Law. We launched the Spring Festival Gala in Rural Areas program both online and offline with the participation of 88 rural spring festival galas from 24 provinces (including prefectures and municipalities), attracting 13.205 million audience attendances online. We also launched a program to collect and present fine art works to depict the well-off life of the people, and the Internet Celebrity from Villages incubation program to encourage and celebrate civility and good manners in rural areas. Major cultural and tourism volunteering projects such as Spring Rain and Sunshine projects were continued to be carried out. We organized the program of "Yangshipin (China Media Group Mobile): A Special Train of Cultural Volunteer" to promote cultural wealth and tourism attractions of poverty-stricken areas. We also pushed forward the work to revise the national standards of public services, including that for evaluating toilets in tourist sites. Throughout the year, 20,300 toilets were built or renovated for tourists, meaning that we overfulfilled the goal of our three-year plan. The work to publish an e-map for tourist toilets was accelerated, with 145,000 toilets marked at various apps.

(1) Public Libraries[4]

By the end of the year, there were in total 3,212 libraries nationwide, 16 more than the number of the previous year. The total number of employees of public libraries across China reached

57,980, 184 more than the number of the previous year. Among them, 7,053 owned senior professional titles, accounting for 12.2%, and 18,868 owned medium-level professional titles, accounting for 32.5%.

According to statistics at the end of 2020, the actual floor space used by public library buildings totaled 17.8577 million m^2, up by 12.2% over the end of the previous year. 1.1792999 billion books[5] were collected in these libraries, up by 6.1%. The number of seats in reading rooms was 1.2647 million, up by 6.2%, and that of computers was 226,234, 419 more than that of the previous year, and that of electronic reading terminals for readers was 143,714, 2022 less than that of the previous year.

By the end of the 2020, the floor space of public libraries for each ten thousand persons was 126.49 m^2, an increase of 5.09 m^2 over the end of the previous year; the number of books per capita was 0.84, an increase of 0.05 over the previous year; the money spent on books per capita was 1.60 yuan, a decrease of 0.08 yuan over previous year.

Figure 1: Information of per capita resource of national public libraries in 2011-2020

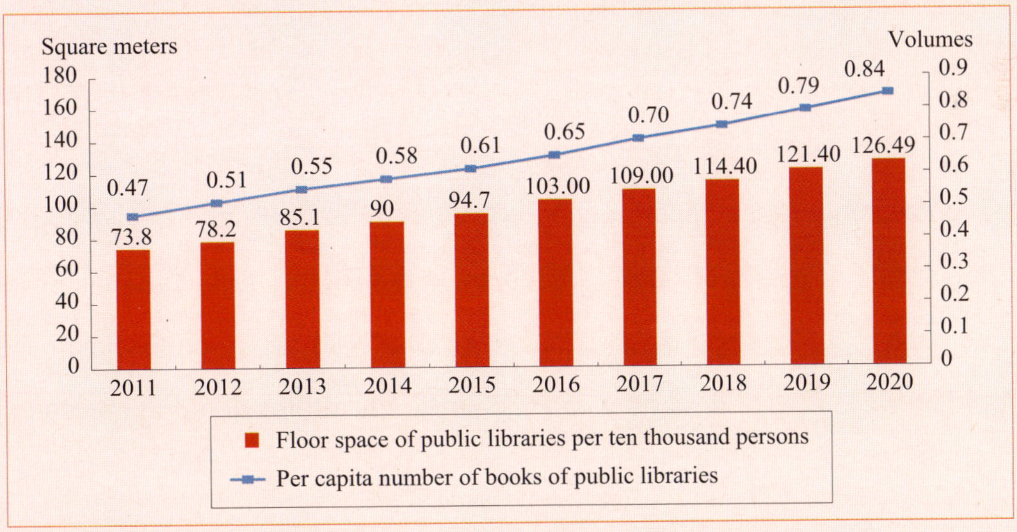

In 2020, library cards issued[6] by public libraries across the country throughout the year total to 102.5131 million, increased by 18.8%; the total flow[7] of person-time reached 541.4581 million, dropping by 39.9%. The total circulation number of books, magazines, and documents loaned to readers reached 420.8715 million, down by 31.4%; readers borrowed books for a total of 174.6662 million times, 34.4% less than the number of previous year. The number of various activities organized for readers totaled 150,713, down by 23.0%, which attracted 92.7933 million attendances, a decrease of 21.3%.

Figure 2: Total flow of person-time and number of books lent out of national public libraries in 2011-2020

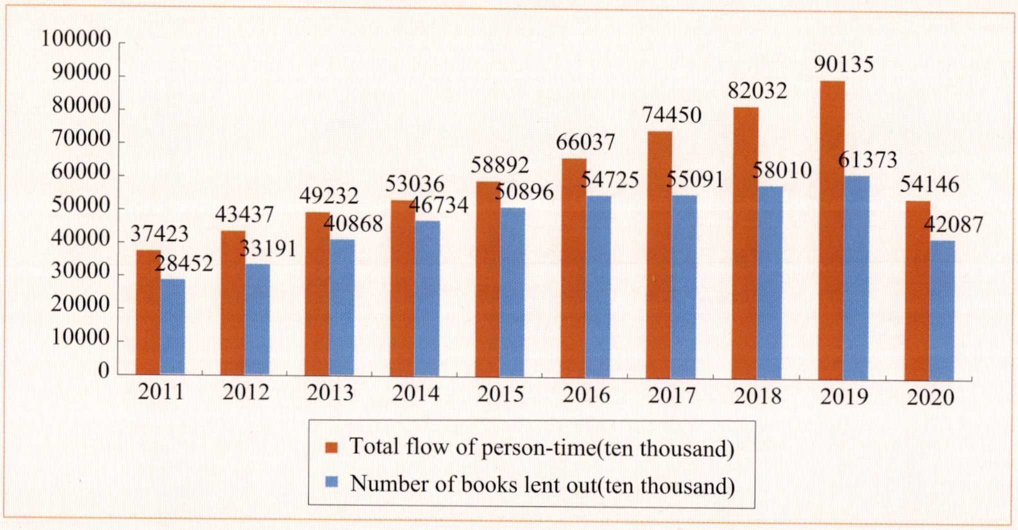

By the end of the year 2020, 2,397 counties (cities/districts at the same level) opened branches of major libraries, and 406 public libraries established management councils.

(2) Public and community cultural institutions[8]

There were a total of 43,687 public and community cultural institutions across the country by the end of 2020, a decrease of 386 over the number of the previous year. Among these, township-level comprehensive cultural stations reached a total of 32,825, a decrease of 705. By the end of the year, the total employees of public and community cultural institutions nationwide reached 185,076 a decrease of 4,992 since the previous year. Staff with senior professional titles reached 7,075, accounting for 3.8%; and staffs with medium-grade professional titles reached 17,969, accounting for 9.7%.

By the end of the year, the actual floor space used by public and community institutions was 46,778,800m^2, up by 3.5% since the previous year; among them, the floor space used for offering public services was 33,878,600m^2, up by 2.8%. By the end of the year, the area covered by cultural facilities for every ten thousand people reached 331.32 m^2, an increase of 2.67% since the previous year.

Figure 3: Area of structure of national cultural facilities of mass per ten thousand people in 2011-2020

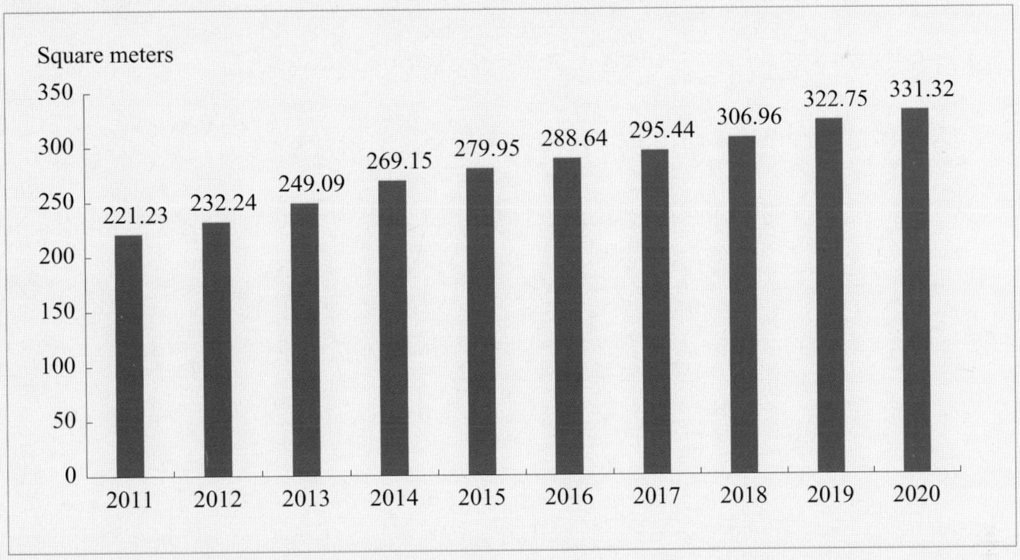

The number of activities[9] organized by nationwide public and community cultural institutions throughout the year reached 1,926,500, down by 21.4% since the previous year; they provided services for 563.2704 million times, down by 28.4%.

By the end of the year, public and community cultural institutions[10] nationwide fostered a total of 9,489 cultural and arts organizations under cultural centers, which presented 120,800 performances to a total audience of 66,758,400. The number of amateur cultural and arts organizations supported by cultural centers (stations) totaled to 454,600, and senior citizen's community colleges set up by cultural centers reached a total of 698.

Table 2: Information of activities organized by nationwide public and community cultural institutions in 2020

	Gross		Increase over previous year (%)	
	Number of activity (ten thousand)	Number of participants (ten thousand person-time)	Number of activity	Person-time of participants
Aggregate of activities	**192.65**	**56327.04**	**-21.4**	**-28.4**
#Cultural activities	108.89	43134.40	-19.9	-28.3
Training class	66.89	3931.26	-24.8	-27.3
Exhibition	13.79	8692.36	-15.9	-30.3
Public lecture	3.06	565.74	-20.2	-20.4

By the end of the year 2020, 575,384 villages set up their own comprehensive cultural service centers, 2,578 counties (cities/districts at the same level) opened branches of major cultural centers, and 394 cultural centers established management councils.

IV. Marketing management and development

In 2020, the Ministry of Culture and Tourism further encouraged culture-related businesses to improve services and image-building. As its endeavor to further upgrade market supervision based on solid policies, the Ministry drafted regulative documents such as the interim regulation for online for-profit tourism services and the notice on deepen the reform to streamline the government, delegate power, and improve government services for the benefit of performing arts market. We revised and published the guidelines of regulating performing arts businesses, built and improved a mechanism for karaoke businesses to self-check their music and repertoire, launched an internet-based tool to check the content of game consoles as well as keep track of the consoles by electronic tags. We improved the tourist safety management systems and mechanisms, organized 2020 safe travel online training course, and provided guidance to more than 40 emergency trainings and drills carried out by local cultural and tourism departments as well as enterprises, with the participation of about 30,000 trainees. The new regulatory mechanism for cultural and tourism markets was further improved, which was based on credibility. We conducted an in-depth research on credibility evaluation system, updated the dishonesty list of cultural and tourism businesses in a regular way, urged the improvement of services provided by cultural businesses, implemented the program to improve the quality of travel-related services, and engaged third-party evaluation so as to further upgrade the efficiency of policies. We also pushed ahead the standardization of hospitality business, and developed a more adequate system to award stars to hotels. We organized the national tour guide qualification examination and high-level and medium-level skill tests for tour guides, and launched a program to help build capacity for professional tour guides.

By the end of the year, business units in the nationwide cultural market[11] reached 208,900, with 1,609,100 employees. There were 65,400 entertainment venues across the country, with 532,300 employees in total. Throughout the year, the sales of business units in the nationwide cultural market reached 996.749 billion yuan, with a profit of 169.97 billion yuan, whereas the numbers for entertainment venues were 41.925 billion yuan and 533 million yuan respectively. The number of internet cafes reached 106,200, with 247,100 employees. Their sales totaled 18.153 billion yuan. Across the country, there were 22,300 performing arts business units with 495,200 employees. Their total sales were 215.75 billion yuan, with a profit of 35.115 billion yuan. There were 5,300 art dealers with 19,400 employees. Their total sales were 7.199 billion yuan, with a profit of 929 million yuan. There were in total 9,700 art dealers with 31,490 employees. Their total sales reached 713.722 billion yuan, with a profit of 133.113 billion yuan.

According to the statistics of 31,074 travel agencies, their total sales in 2020 reached 238.969 billion yuan, with a profit of 6.915 billion yuan. They directly employed 322,500 people.

According to the statistics of 8,423 star hotels, their total sales in 2020 reached 122.153 billion yuan, with the average daily rate (ADR) of 313.91 yuan room/night and the average occupancy rate of 39.0%.

In 2020, the Ministry deepened the cultural market comprehensive policing reform to strengthen policing over cultural, antique, publishing, radio, TV, film and tourism markets with the focus on streamlining and reorganizing cultural market policing task force. All provinces, autonomous regions and municipalities in China have published practical measures of reform, and all provincial cultural and tourism administrations have established supervision departments or divisions in charge of cultural market policing at provincial level. Across China, 99.8% of the cities (and municipal-level prefectures and leagues) have merged their cultural and tourism market policing task forces, 85.5% of them merged their district-level task forces into city-level ones, 4.1% of them dismissed their city-level task forces but kept the district-level ones; 95.9% of the counties (and township level cities and districts) have merged their cultural and tourism market policing task forces, and incorporate the administration of these task forces into the responsibility of cultural market supervision departments. Throughout the year, we organized 25 workshops online and offline to train more than 30,000 people, guided and supervised 9 local policing task force job tests and completed the documentation of the qualification certificates and identifications of 4,239 professionals.

In 2020, further steps were made to step up market policing and regulation, including four rounds of unannounced checks and evaluations over cultural and tourism businesses across the country. In cooperation with departments including the Cyberspace Administration of China, we carried out a special action to regulate the live streaming business, and check the live streaming apps that allowed users to upload art performances. We investigated and penalized internet-based cultural businesses that offered illegal cultural activities and banned contents in violation of relevant laws and regulations. We commanded more than 470,000 rounds of task force patrol around tourist sites nationwide and solved more than 1,100 problems on site as our efforts to improve policing over travel industry, especially on holidays. We conducted strict regulation of livestream sales of tourism products, and investigated and penalized more than 30 travel agencies and online shops that violated the regulation. We also prosecuted a series of representative cases which involved the travel industry. 87 cases of cultural market policing were identified as major cases of the years 2019-2020. In cooperation with the Publicity Department of the CPC Central Committee, The Ministry of Public Security and the Supreme People's Procuratorate of China, we supervised the prosecution of 42 major cases with adverse social impact. We continued to encourage the use of the technical monitor and online service platform for cultural market policing. Throughout the year, 8,827 complaints were filed on the platform, among which 6,725 were solved. 316,410,000 daily checks were initiated, and 10.8894 million professionals were dispatched for such checks. 20,900 new cases were prosecuted, and 28,400 were closed so far.

V. Resource Development

In 2020, the Ministry established a leading group to guide the national census of China's cultural resources, drafted a plan for building China's public database of cultural resources and technical specifications of national tourism resource census, and launched the role model programs to facilitate cultural and tourism resource census. 22 new national-level 5A tourist sites and 15 new national-level holiday resorts were authenticated, the lists of 71 new national-level all-for-one tourism role model zones and 680 national-level role model villages for rural tourism were published. We launched several nationwide tourism promotions, including the ones focusing on autumn and winter tourism, outdoor experience, ice and snow tourism, and self-drive tours. We also supported the trans-regional themed promotions carried out by Yellow River, the Great Wall and Yangtze River tourism promotion alliances.

In response to the Covid-19 pandemic, we offered “rural tourism face-to-face” live streaming courses, which ran for 49 sessions with more than 700,000 views. We commissioned and published the handbook of self-drive tours around "three regions and three prefectures" (the "three regions" refers to Tibet; four prefectures of southern Xinjiang: Hotan, Aksu, Kashi and the Kirgiz Autonomous Prefecture of Kizilsu; and areas in Sichuan, Yunnan, Gansu, and Qinghai provinces with large Tibetan populations. The "three prefectures" are Liangshan in Sichuan, Nujiang in Yunnan, and Linxia in Gansu), arranged a special train to help bring tourists who visited "three regions and three prefectures" to farther destinations in Tibet. Further efforts were made to help people in poverty with tourism, as 22,600 villages with one-on-one aid from the tourism sector were all lifted out of poverty. Tourism related to revolutionary heritage of China (red tourism) witnessed steady growth, as we launched various events and programs including the capacity building program for outstanding tour guides of red tourism, a showcase of best practices in boosting red tourism, the 10th contest of red tourism package planning for college students, 2020 China Red Tourism Exposition, red tourism online course and a red tourism promotion in collaboration with Xinjiang Production Construction Corps (XPCC).

By the end of this year, there were 13,332 A-level tourist sites in China, an increase of 930

Table 4: Domestic tourism developinent in 2011-2020

since the previous year. Among them, 302 were 5A-level sites, 22 more than that of the previous year, 4030 were at 4A-level, up by 310, and 6,931 were at 3A-level, up by 733.

Throughout the year, 2.879 billion domestic visits were made, decreasing by 52.1% over that of the previous year. The revenue of domestic tourism totaled 2.23 trillion yuan, dropping by 61.1% over that of the previous year.

VI. Cultural and Tourism Industries and Related Technology

In 2020, as its active effort to foster new forms of business and consumption, the Ministry of Culture and Tourism formulated and published the opinion on promoting the high-quality growth of digital cultural industry, and published in collaboration with other departments including the National Development and Reform Commission (NDRC) the opinions on expanding and upgrading consumption to boost a robust domestic market, and on fostering healthy development of new forms of business and consumption to boost consumption and employment. We also joined NDRC and the Ministry of Finance to publish the lists of 15 national-level role model cities and 60 pilot cities in which we encouraged citizens to spend more on culture and tourism.

In 2020, the Ministry of Culture and Tourism authenticated 9 new National Role Model Parks for Cultural Industry and approved applications from 18 parks to build themselves into Role Model Park. By the end of the year, there were in total 19 National Role Model Parks for Cultural Industry. The Ministry also worked with other departments including the Ministry of Industry and Information Technology to formulate and publish Several Opinions on the Improvement of the Supporting Mechanism for SME Development.

We joined six financing institutions including the China Development Bank to select 320 cultural and tourism investment and financing projects with the total investment of 619.41 billion yuan. Matchmaking events were organized, including 7 focusing on key projects and one for the Grand Canal related projects, to successfully matched 452 projects with the total investment of 340.59 billion yuan. To help bail out the cultural and tourism businesses heavily hit by the pandemic, the Ministry also signed an agreement with ICBC, and the latter provided 100 billion yuan in financing and credit to those businesses. With the support of China UnionPay, we upgraded the technical facilities in 24,000 cultural and tourist sites for consumers to pay by mobile phone. We hosted the Belt and Road Forum on International Cooperation in Cultural and Tourism Industries, the 13th China-Japan-ROK Cultural Industries Forum, and collected initiatives concerning Belt and Road international cooperation in cultural and tourism business sectors, and selected 45 key programs as recipient of our support.

According to the National Bureau of Statistics, in 2020, the total turnover of major cultural and culture related businesses reached 9851.4 billion yuan, increasing by 2.2% over that of the previous year on comparable basis.

In 2020, the Ministry of Culture and Tourism completed the work to select qualified nominees for the "technology for economy 2020" national key project, the national cultural and tourism technology innovation project and the Ministry's project to subsidize key laboratories. The laboratory of the Palace Museum was approved to be enlisted in the second list of "Belt and Road" collaborative laboratories issued by the Ministry of Science and Technology. We published 13 national and trade standards in cultural and tourism sectors, as well as the fourth list of role model institutions of tourist service standardization. By the end of 2020, there were in total 198 such institutions. We accelerated the work to integrate online government service platforms of the Ministry and pilot provinces, initiated 242 new art-related projects to apply for the National Social Science Fund of China, encouraged the research on cultural heritage of the Yellow River and Yangtze river, and organized activities including student art and creativity exhibitions in art vocational schools nationwide.

VII. Cultural Heritage Conservation and Management

In 2020, further steps were taken to implement the opinions on further promoting reform of heritage preservation and exploitation, the opinions on implementing the project to protect and make good use of revolutionary relics (2018-2022), and the guiding opinions on improving preservation and exploitation of grotto temples. We improved the management systems for immovable cultural heritage and heritage preservation projects, pushed ahead the project aimed at tracing the origins of Chinese civilization, the key archaeological projects of China and researches on Chinese nation's cultural genes, as well as initiated the the second phase of archaeological and cultural heritage protection projects along the east front of South-to-North water diversion project.

National Cultural Heritage Administration made further efforts to preserve and make good use of revolutionary heritage, including publishing the second list of 22 preservation areas, which covered 988 counties of 228 cities in 31 provinces across China; urging local cultural administrations to draft special plans and publish inventories; facilitating related programs by giving approvals and advice to 246 programs to preserve first level revolutionary heritage sites and items, and organizing events such as "online Wuhan revolutionary heritage month" and "following the footsteps of the martyrs". According to our census, there were in total more than 2.7 million ancient books and manuscripts written in Han dialect.

By the end of the year, there were 11,314 cultural heritage institutions all over China, an increase of 752 over the number of previous year. Among these, 3,373 were for the preservation of cultural relics, accounting for 29.8%; and 5,452 were museums[12], accounting for 48.2%. By the end of the year, the number of employees by cultural heritage institutions reached 175,800, 13,400 more than the number of the previous year. Among them, 11,072 were with senior professional titles, accounting for 6.3%; and 22,165 were with medium-grade professional titles, accounting for 12.6%.

By the end of the year, there were 50.891 million items of collections of cultural relics in the

Figure 5: Information of national cultural relics agencies and employed persons in 2011-2020

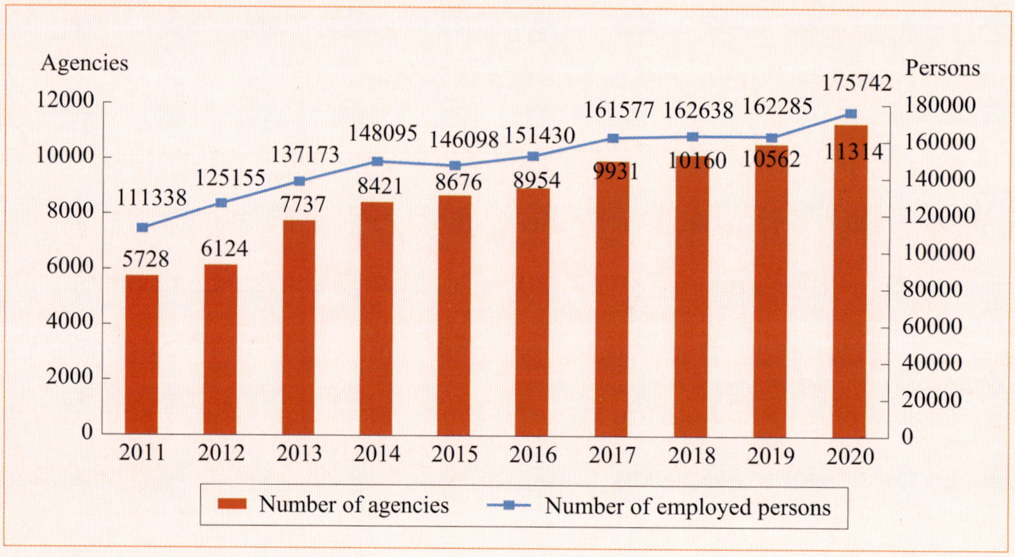

cultural heritage institutions. Among these, the amount of collections in museums totaled to 43.1909 million, which accounted for 84.9% of the total.

In 2020, 28,924 exhibitions were displayed across the country, 1778 less than those of the previous year. Throughout the year, the number of nationwide basic exhibitions arranged by cultural heritage institutions[13] reached 16,259, increased by 1,235 over that of the previous year; and temporary exhibitions[14] totaled 12,665, decreased by 3,013; the number of visitor attendances dropped to 616.317 million, which was a decrease of 53.2% over that of the previous year. Among these, 526.5235 million visits were to museums, accounting for 85.4% of the total visits to cultural heritage institutions, down by 53.1%. Among the visitors, the number of minors was 135.6408 million, dropping by 57.1%, accounting for 22.0% of all visitors.

In 2020, Taijiquan and Ong Chun/Wangchuan/Wangkang ceremony, rituals and related

Figure 6: Person-time of audiences and minors cultural relic agencies accepting in 2011-2020

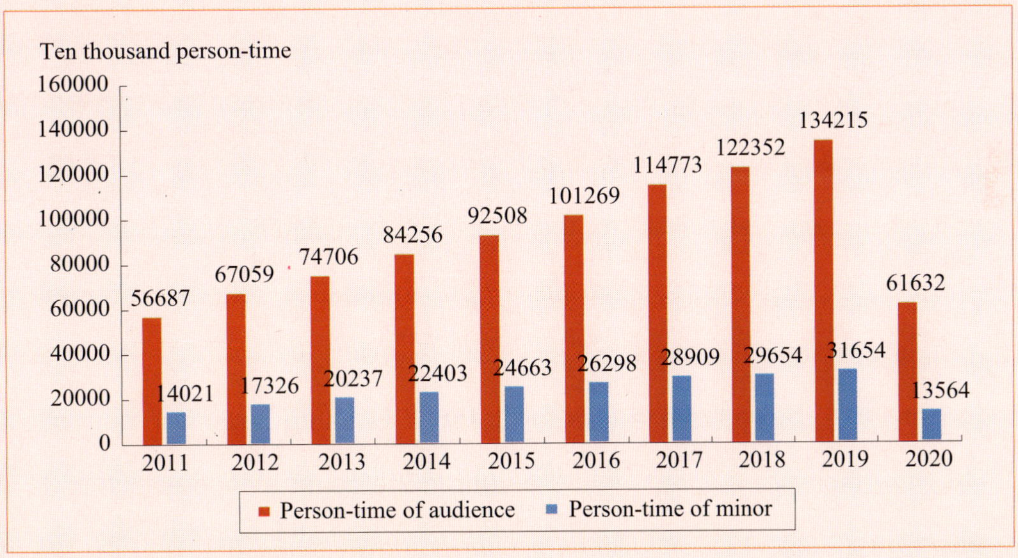

practices for maintaining the sustainable connection between man and the ocean were inscribed on the UNESCO on the Representative List of the Intangible Cultural Heritage of Humanity. Steady progresses were made in the work to nominate Ancient Tea Plantations of Jingmai Mountain in Pu'er, Maritime Silk Road, Silk Roads in South Asia and great tea road that spanned China, Mongolia and Russia for inscription on the World Heritage List. The Ministry completed the preliminary evaluation of the elements to be inscribed on the fifth national representative list of the intangible cultural heritage (ICH), and regulated the work to safeguard the ICH elements on the UNESCO List. Further efforts were made to implement the traditional craftsmanship revitalization plan, carry out the ICH bearer capacity building program and the measures to recognize and manage bearers of ICH elements on the national list, as we documented 249 such bears. We set up the coordination mechanism to safeguard ICH along the Yellow River and the Grand Canal, organized the ICH survey along the Yellow River, set up around 40 pilot ICH-based quyi (traditional local opera) houses, and established pilot zones to preserve cultural environments of Heluo culture and Jingdezhen porcelain culture. We held the 6th China Intangible Cultural Heritage Expo, the 2020 "Cultural and Natural Heritage Day" ICH presentations, "National ICH Quyi Week", and ICH showcases to celebrate the Chinese New Year. We also supported local governments and institutions to organize ICH trade fairs, as well as brand events including Hangzhou craftsmanship week and the first China Textile Intangible Cultural Heritage Conference. We encouraged schools, communities and tourist sites to present and promote ICH, and recommended 12 ICH routes across the country to tourists.

By the end of 2020, there were 3,068 national-level representative intangible cultural heritage (ICH) bearers recognized by the Ministry of Culture and Tourism and 1,372 national-level representative ICH elements endorsed by the State Council. There were 42 Chinese elements inscribed on the UNESCO Representative List of the Intangible Cultural Heritage of Humanity, more than any other countries in the world.

By the end of 2020, there were a total of 2,455 ICH safeguarding institutions across the country, with 16,444 employees. Throughout the year in the country, these institutions held 56,117 showcases, down by 22.0%, 12,227 folklore activities, down by 28.0%, and 16,174 exhibitions, down by 17.4%.

VIII. International Cultural and Tourism Exchange and Bonding with Hong Kong, Macao and Taiwan Regions

In 2020, The Ministry of Culture and Tourism continued to foster the Belt and Road international cooperation by organizing a livestream show which gathered worldwide artists, an online relay of global museums to showcase their treasures, an exhibition of the manuscripts and documents related to the Silk Road, etc. We deepened bilateral cooperation in an all-round way by exchanging ministerial visits with other countries, holding 16 high-level meetings, signing executive programs of cooperation or MOUs with 7 countries such as Hungary and Greece, celebrating anniversaries of diplomatic ties with 6 countries including Italy and Saudi Arabia and offering capacity building programs to Nigeria and other 7 African countries. We also participated in 32 major online conferences including the cultural ministers' meeting of the BRICS, G20 and UNESCO and steadily pushed forward the construction of the World Tourism Alliance's headquarters.

The Ministry of Culture and Tourism continued to be committed to Beautiful China promotion, as we worked to present a true, multi-dimensional and panoramic view of China through over 2,200 activities. We organized around 200 Happy Chinese New Year celebrative events, participated in in international expos such as Online Tourism Expo Japan and World Travel Market London, as well as organized online exchange activities including a virtual concert themed "Silk Road" in cooperation with related countries and a online forum on contemporary music with Asian and African countries. We coordinated and guided the work of overseas China Cultural Centers and Tourism Offices to carry out online programs including the virtual tours around China and Mid-Autumn Festival cultural week.

The Ministry continued to deepen cultural and tourism bonding with Hong Kong, Macao and Taiwan, published a plan for cultural and tourism development in the Guangdong-Hong Kong-Macao Greater Bay Area (GBA), and held online symposiums on cross-strait tourism and cultural exchanges. We hosted cultural events including the national performing arts troupe show season in Macao, an exhibition of documents and archives to commemorate the 75th anniversary of Taiwan's recovery from Japanese occupation, Yihailiujin (literally, interflow across the golden sea of arts) cultural tour in Anhui province, and the online cross-strait cultural and tourism dialogue with the nature and culture of Qinghai province as the theme. As our efforts to further promote the brand cultural events in Hong Kong, Macao and Taiwan, we also organized youth programs such as one to offer opportunities to young people of Hong Kong and Macao to know more about the Chinese mainland, and one to familiarize Taiwan youths with the Chinese New Year traditions, as well as launched the study tour alliance conference to encourage youths of Hong Kong and Macao to take cultural tours and study tours in Chinese mainland.

In 2020, we opened three new China Cultural Centers in Hungary, Jordan and Kuwait respectively. By the end of the year, there were in total 45 overseas China Cultural Centers and 20 Chinese tourism offices in foreign countries. Moreover, we also have established the Asia Tourism Exchange Center in Hong Kong, and the offices of Association For Tourism Exchange Across The Taiwan Straits in Taipei and Gaoxiong. Throughout the year, cultural and art troupes made 947 attendances and 12,552 persons have participated in the international cultural exchange programs and cultural bonding programs with Hong Kong, Macao and Taiwan.

IX. Investment

In 2020, the Ministry of Culture and Tourism fulfilled a budget of 5.951 billion yuan and transfer payments of 5.492 billion yuan as the central budget's subsidy to local governments. The Ministry took the full-coverage audit and performance management measure to improve the efficiency of the utilization of funds and assets. There were steady progresses in major cultural infrastructure projects, such as the construction of buildings of the National Art Museum of China and the China Arts and Crafts Museum (tentative name), as well as the Forbidden City in Safety program.

Figure 7: National cultural and tourism undertaking expenses per capita (2011-2020)

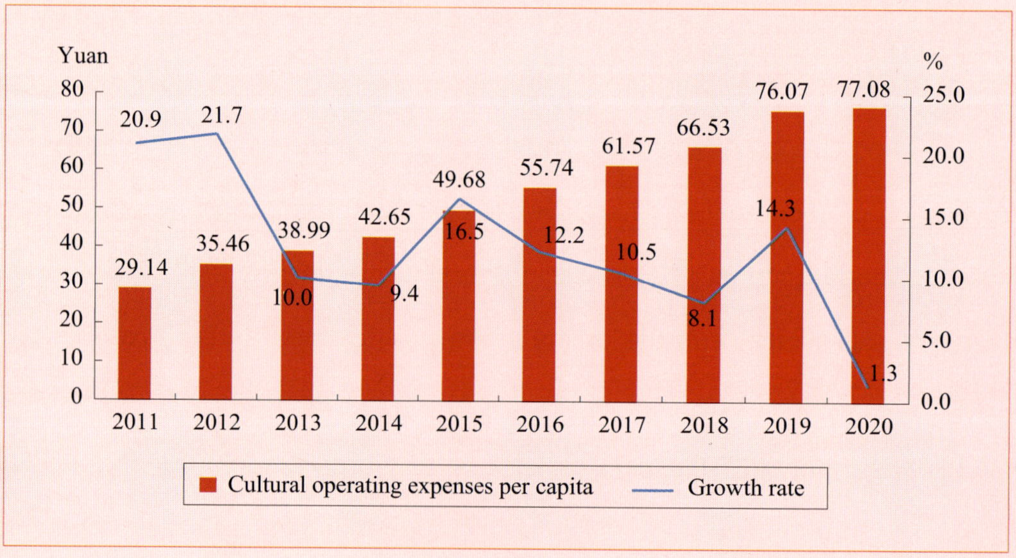

The total amount of cultural and tourism undertaking expenses[15] for the whole year was 108.826 billion yuan, an increase of 22.5 billion yuan over that of the previous year, up by 2.1%; as for the national cultural and tourism undertaking expenses per capita, the total was 77.08 yuan, an increase of 1.01 yuan over the previous year, up by 1.3%.

Regarding the national cultural and tourism undertaking expenses, that of cultural and tourism units above county level was 50.098 billion yuan, accounting for 46.0%, 2.5 percentage points lower than that of the previous year; that of cultural and tourism units of county level or below the level of county was 58.728 billion yuan, accounting for 54.0%, up by 2.5 percentage points in the

Table 3: Urban & Rural and Regional-based distribution of national cultural undertaking expenses

		In 1995	In 2000	In 2005	In 2010	In 2015	In 2018	In 2019	In 2020
Aggregate (one hundred million yuan)	**Nationwide**	**33.4**	**63.2**	**133.8**	**323.1**	**686.0**	**928.3**	**1065.8**	**1088.3**
	# Above county level	24.4	46.3	98.1	206.7	352.8	425.0	517.7	501.0
	County level and below level of county	9.0	16.9	35.7	116.4	330.1	503.4	548.1	587.3
	# Eastern region	13.4	28.9	64.4	143.4	287.9	416.2	478.2	491.6
	Central region	9.5	15.1	30.6	78.7	164.3	232.7	265.3	269.8
	Western region	8.3	13.7	27.6	85.8	193.9	242.9	278.0	301.6
Proportion (%)	**Nationwide**	**100.0**	**100.0**	**100.0**	**100.0**	**100.0**	**100.0**	**100.0**	**100.0**
	# Above county level	73.2	73.4	73.3	64.0	51.7	45.8	48.5	46.0
	County level and below level of county	26.8	26.7	26.7	36.0	48.3	54.2	51.5	54.0
	# Eastern region	40.2	45.7	48.1	44.4	42.1	44.8	44.9	45.1
	Central region	28.6	23.8	22.9	24.3	24.1	25.1	24.9	24.8
	Western region	24.9	21.7	20.6	26.6	28.4	26.2	26.1	27.7

sense of its proportion. The cultural and tourism undertaking expenses of eastern region[16] reached 49.162 billion yuan, accounting for 45.1%, and its proportion increased by 0.2%; that of central region reached 26.978 billion yuan, accounting for 24.8%, its proportion decreased by 0.1%; and that of western region reached 30.164 billion yuan, accounting for 27.7%, 1.6 percentage points higher than the number of the previous year.

The amount of maintenance expenses of national cultural heritage[17] was 40.020 billion yuan, a decrease of 1.521 billion yuan, or 3.7% over that of the previous year.

Notes:

[1] All the data of the communiqué are preliminary statistical data. HKSAR, MSAR, and Taiwan Province are not included in each data. Some of data are not compatible with the total of subentries due to rounding off.

[2] Cultural and tourism units refers to cultural institutions that national cultural and tourism departments of all levels organize or implement industrial management, excluding cultural institutions organized or managed by the departments of all levels of press and publications, radio , film and television, etc. According to the current statistical system, the cultural institutions (such as public libraries, cultural centers, cultural stations, museums, etc.) organized by cultural departments are brought into the statistical range. Regarding cultural institutions with industrial management, the private art performance troupes, cybercafé, and entertainment venues are brought into statistical range, while the mechanism of exchange of works of art, internet culture institution are not in the range.

[3] The art performance troupes mean various professional artistic performance organizations which are organized by cultural and tourism institutions or to which the cultural institutions implement industrial management (with approval of cultural administration department and commercial performance license), and is engaged in such activities as performing arts.

[4] Public library refers to all kinds of institutions that are organized by cultural departments at all levels, and is open to public as well as providing popularization and education of science, culture, and other knowledge.

[5] The total collection of books in public libraries refers to the sum of audiovisual literature materials including bound volume, manual, manuscript, micro-reproduction, videotape, audio tape and CD of ancient books, books, periodicals and newspapers in catalogue. It does not include digital books.

[6] The number of library cards issued refers to the number of library cards which are issued by public libraries and used at least once in that very year.

[7] The total flow of person-time of public library refers to the gross person-time of receiving the service of the libraries in that year, including borrowing books, consultation and participating in

various readers' activities.

[8] The mass cultural institutions refer to the places that cultural departments at all levels organize for mass cultural activities, mainly including cultural centers (including comprehensive cultural center and mass art gallery) and cultural stations.

[9] That the mass cultural institution organizes and carries out activities means the sum of the organizations of cultural literary and artistic activities, training classes, exhibitions, and public lectures.

[10] The literature and art organizations of mass cultural institutions refer to performance teams composed by the staff of this institution and that provide performances for the mass.

[11] The operating units of cultural markets refer to the agencies which are approved or filed by administrative departments of cultural markets and have relevant licenses and filing documents, and that engage in cultural management and services. In line with the current statistical systems, the statistical range of operating units of the cultural market only include private art performance troupes, entertainment venues, and business sites of internet access services.

[12] The museum refers to the non-profit and permanent social service institution which collects, preserves, and exhibits the witness of human activity and natural environment with intent of research, education, and appreciation, as well as being open to the public. It includes the units that carry out activities with proper names such as museums, memorial halls, science and technology museums, exhibition halls, etc.

[13] Basic exhibition refers to the exhibition which is displayed in the pavilion, with fixed location and for an extended time.

[14] Temporary exhibition means the multi-formed exhibition which is set in the institution and designed by the pavilion.

[15] Cultural operating expense means aggregate of expenditures that the finance of all levels in the area invests to the organizer of cultural systems. It generally includes financial appropriation (excluding appropriations of capital construction costs) of cultural institutions such as art performance troupes, public libraries, cultural centers (stations), etc. and financial subsidies of enterprises subordinate to the Ministry of Culture. According to current statistical caliber, cultural

operating expense does not include administrative operation expenditures of cultural administration and management departments at all levels.

[16] Eastern region includes Beijing, Tianjin, Liaoning Province, Shanghai, Jiangsu Province, Fujian Province, Shandong Province, and Guangdong Province; Central region includes Hebei Province, Shanxi Province, Jilin Province, Heilongjiang Province, Anhui Province, Jiangxi Province, Henan Province, Hubei Province, Hunan Province and Hainan Province; Western region includes Inner Mongolia (autonomous region), Guangxi Province, Chongqing, Sichuan Province, Guizhou Province, Yunan Province, Tibet (autonomous region), Shaanxi Province, Gansu Province, Qinghai Province, Ningxia (autonomous region), and Xinjiang (autonomous region).

[17] Operating expenses of cultural relics refer to the aggregate of expenditures that the finance departments at all levels in the area invest to the operation of cultural relics. It generally includes financial appropriation (excluding appropriation of capital construction) of operation institutions of cultural relic such as museum, protection and management agencies for cultural relics, etc. and financial subsidies of enterprises subordinate to cultural relic departments.